Ancient Magick for
Today's Witch Series

GYPSY MAGIC

MONIQUE JOINER SIEDLAK

oshunpublications.com

Gypsy Magic © Copyright 2019 Monique Joiner Siedlak

ISBN 978-1-948834-96-4 (Paperback)

ISBN 978-1-948834-92-6 (eBook)

All rights reserved

The content contained within this book may not be reproduced, duplicated or transmitted without direct written permission from the author or the publisher.

Under no circumstances will any blame or legal responsibility be held against the publisher, or author, for any damages, reparation, or monetary loss due to the information contained within this book, either directly or indirectly.

Legal Notice

This book is copyright protected. It is only for personal use. You cannot amend, distribute, sell, use, quote or paraphrase any part, or the content within this book, without the consent of the author or publisher.

Disclaimer Notice

Please note the information contained within this document is for educational and entertainment purposes only. All effort has been executed to present accurate, up to date, reliable, complete information. No warranties of any kind are declared or implied. Readers acknowledge that the author is not engaged in the rendering of legal, financial, medical or professional advice. The content within this book has been derived from various sources. Please consult a licensed professional before attempting any techniques outlined in this book.

By reading this document, the reader agrees that under no circumstances is the author responsible for any losses, direct or indirect, that are incurred as a result of the use of the information contained within this document, including, but not limited to, errors, omissions, or inaccuracies.

Cover Design by MJS

Cover Images by MidJourney

Published by Oshun Publications

www.oshunpublications.com

ANCIENT MAGICK FOR TODAY'S WITCH SERIES

The *Ancient Magick for Today's Witch Series* is a series for modern witches to explore ancient magick, covering Celtic, Gypsy, and Crystal magic, among others. It offers practical advice on spells, rituals, and enchantments for today's use, incorporating natural energies and spiritual connections. With insights into Shamanism, Wicca, and more, it helps readers enhance their magickal journey, offering paths to protection, prosperity, and spiritual growth by combining ancient wisdom with contemporary practice.

Wiccan Basics

Candle Magick

Wiccan Spells

Love Spells

Abundance Spells

Herb Magick

Moon Magick

Creating Your Own Spells

Gypsy Magic

Protection Magick

Celtic Magick

Shamanic Magick

Crystal Magic

Sacred Spaces

Solitary Witchcraft

Novice Witch's Guide

MONIQUE JOINER SIEDLAK

GET UPDATES, FREEBIES & GIVEAWAYS

JOIN MY NEWSLETTER

MOJOSIEDLAK.COM/MOONLIGHT-MUSINGS

CONTENTS

1. The Incredible Roma History — 1
2. Roma Customs and Religion — 5
3. Gypsy Lore of the Roma People — 9
4. Gypsy Divination — 13
5. Amulets, Charms, and Talismans — 47
6. Simple Spells — 55
7. Gypsy Superstitions — 61
8. International Romani Day — 65

Glossary Terms — 69
About the Author — 73
More Books by Monique — 75
Don't Miss Out — 79

1

THE INCREDIBLE ROMA HISTORY

If you are looking for fascinating history, then the incredible Roma history is just what you need to know about. The Romani people are Europe's largest minority group who had migrated from northwest India some 1500 years ago as can be told from new genetic studies. The Romani people are also known as Roma who was previously referred to as Gypsies in the 16th century due to their group being widely dispersed.

Some people also thought that the Roma were from Egypt. These days, the term gypsy is considered to be derogatory and hence, is not used. Thanks to the advent of genetic technology, researchers have been able to analyze the genetic history of most of Europe and found different accounts of migration groups such as the history of the Jewish Diaspora which is considered to be one of the biggest and interesting.

Genetic Studies

There are considered to be 11 million Roma people in Europe. However, their history has been neglected throughout the years. Genetic studies already suggest that the Roma people hail from North-Eastern Pakistan and North-Western India. Their DNA samples have been taken throughout Europe and their genes from that they are initially from South Asia.

Different techniques have been used to uncover the history of the Roma people and DNA samples of up to 13 groups of the Roma people have been taken throughout Europe to learn more about the people. The genome as a whole has been studied to find complete genetic information about the Roma population spread out within Europe.

Migrated At the Same Time

The results of the various studies and research suggest that modern Roma ancestors had migrated all at once from North-Eastern Pakistan and North-Western India about 1,500 years ago. When the Roma people arrived in Europe, they quickly spread out within the European continent from the Balkan region to just about every area in the continent some 900 years ago.

Intermarriage

Throughout history from when the Roma people first arrived in Europe up until now, the Roma people intermarried with the local population and hence, waned. They were even discriminated during the Holocaust period. It has been said that somewhere between 200,000 to 1,500,000 Roma people had been killed by Hitler's Nazis.

Post World War II

After World War II, the Roma people, especially in communist countries, had been severely targeted for assimilation and that also led to them being forced sterilized to reduce their birth rates. Once the analysis is widened to include more Roma groups, more information can be gathered about the Pakistan and Indian populations from the area where the Roma people had first migrated.

The Roma of Today

Twelve European countries pledged to eliminate prejudice against the Roma through the Decade of Roma Inclusion. The effort concentrated on employment, education, wellness, and housing. Nevertheless, notwithstanding the action, Roma continues to encounter extensive bias.

Today, most Roma have settled down into apartments and houses and are not easily discernible. Roma people use cars instead of horses or wagons as in the past. Because of continuous discrimination, many do not openly acknowledge their origins and only reveal themselves to other Roma.

The almost one million American Roma, fearful of the bigotry, segregation, and violence, keep a low profile. They do not wish to experience what have pained their European equivalents and ancestry for a thousand years and still face daily. Assimilation makes sense to American Roma.

2

ROMA CUSTOMS AND RELIGION

Gypsy Spiritual Beliefs

Gypsies or the Roma people as they referred to as have an extensive history as their ancestors had migrated from North-Eastern Pakistan and North-Western India to Europe some 1500 years ago. These people brought with them their culture and beliefs. Some of these beliefs are spiritual which had dictated their lives and some Roma even adhere to these religious beliefs today.

Belief in Possession

The Gypsy people believe in possession and that a person is under the influence of the Devil when they are possessed. A recurring theme in their spiritual beliefs is that of the Devil, and they acknowledge his existence and that he has sinister intentions. Possession is not necessarily thought of as something evil.

Belief in Werewolves and Vampires

One might be thinking that is it the Gypsies who actually wrote the Twilight series due to their belief in werewolves and vampires. Werewolves and vampires are considered of as something terrible and that vampires are draining spirits which could exist from any negative influences.

Crystals

The Gypsy people have a massive belief in crystals and that they influence just about everything from your daily routine to negative energy. The Gypsy or Roma people have been said to have adopted magic from other cultures and used it as per their understanding of the world. True to their Pakistani and Indian origins, they respect to fire, and it is seen as a symbol for good energy. This is why campfires have been so popular. It is a spiritual belief among the Gypsy people that it isn't just the living beings who gather around the fire but also the dead and impure spirits are thought to be afraid of such fire.

Importance of Music

Music is more than just sound but is a part of the culture of the Gypsy people due to how it impacts a person's spirit. They also believe that a poorly performed song causes bad luck. Possessions are even thought of as to hold power, and due to this the properties of a family member are destroyed, sold to outsiders or thrown away. It is seen as stealing from the dead and is also considered a cause of bad luck. Never covet the possessions of the deceased when in a Gypsy clan.

Dancing is Much More than Just a Fun Activity

One might find dancing to be a great way to exercise or have fun but for the Gypsies, it is a part of their religion, and they can be seen singing hymns and dancing to music. Dance and songs is a sign of good luck and are thought of as a way to uplift and strengthen one's spirit. Only those songs are played or dances performed which are known to bring good luck. If you can't dance, then it is ok, but you should play the drum or sing along with them.

Roma Family Structure

Due to their small size of just about 11 million Gypsies within Europe, the Gypsies are tight-knit and stay connected with their clans.

The Roma communities place a high significance on close family connections and generally serve as the foundation of more essential community groups. Communities typically include members of the extended family residing together. The archetypal Roma family consists of a married couple, their eligible children, and at least a married son, his wife, and their kids.

It's been said though, during the courting stage, girls are encouraged to dress suggestively; sex is a matter that is not had until after the wedding. Some groups have argued that no boy under 17 or girl under 16 will be married.

Still, even though Romani typically marry young, many marriages are arranged. Weddings are frequently very elaborate, involving extremely grand and flashy dress for not only the bride but her many bridesmaids.

Upon marriage, a new couple often lives with the parents of the husband while the young bride learns the particulars of her husband's group. Ideally, by the time an older son is ready to move away with his family, a younger son will have married and joined the home with his new wife. Although the action had diminished considerably by in the past couple of decades, marriages customarily were arranged by the elders in the family to reinforce kinship connections to other families or political bonds.

3

GYPSY LORE OF THE ROMA PEOPLE

The Roma people have been said to migrate from modern-day North-Eastern Pakistan and North-Western India about 1500 years ago. These people migrated to Europe together at the same time and eventually spread out within the European continent. Genetic researches prove this pattern of migration and new studies are being conducted about the group to uncover more secrets.

The groups of Roma people have also been referred to as gypsies due to their dispersive and nomadic nature of life and have faced harsh discrimination especially during the reign of Hitler and the post-World War II communist nations. Many Roma were even sterilized to eliminate the population, but even today about 11 million Roma people can be found in Europe, they might not admit their roots, but they hail from Pakistan and India.

Migration of the Roma People

Due to the movement of the Roma people, they brought with them many things such as their cuisine but most importantly their South Asian culture and lore which is also called gypsy lore by others. South Asia is known for its culture and hospitality, and the Roma still have that sense of hospitality even today despite the years spent in Europe.

Gypsy lore has become a favorite topic among people, especially those who want to learn more about Roma people. The folklore covers just about every subject from astrology to psychology. The gypsy lore had been passed down from generation to generation to teach the newborn about their history and culture. There are many, popular gypsy lore and there even is a Gypsy Lore Society in Liverpool which is dedicated to serving the Roma people and learning more about them. Here is some of the gypsy lore which some people might even believe in today.

Existence of Dragons

Popular gypsy lore is one about the existence of dragons. The gypsies had traveled extensively throughout South Asia, the Caucus Region, and Europe, and because of this fact, people readily accepted the lore which spoke about dragons. Some people even got scared of going to the mountains. Dragons are a favorite topic even today, with many televisions serials and movies depicting dragons just as how they had been first described by the Roma.

The Golden Stag

Another, popular gypsy lore is the tale of the golden stag which is a story of an old woman who tells her husband that he will lose his two children, from his previous marriage, a daughter and a son, while in the woods. During the first time, he went with the children to the woods, they came back. However the second time when they went to the woods, the old man lost them. The children could not find any water until they reached a place where a fox lived. Whose home also had a well for water. The brother had been warned by the sister not to drink the water as it would transform him into a fox. The brother was too thirsty; he finally gave in and drank the water. So, he became the golden stag. The stag lifted his sister up on a tree until one day a prince saw her and immediately fell in love with her. After that, the sister and prince got married.

4
GYPSY DIVINATION

At some time in your life; you had wished you could tell what the future would be like. Admit it, you have. Well, you should know that you are not alone in your thoughts. There is an absolute comfort that comes with knowing how things will turn out - that is why we can reread old books and re-watch old movies and still enjoy them - sometimes even more than the first time. Surprises can be great, but nothing beats foreknowledge.

The desire to know what life has in store for you is a universal feeling, and you just cannot "Que sera sera," your thoughts out of it. This would explain why Gypsy divination is so prevalent today. Gypsies are essentially fortune tellers who practice divination and can make predictions about your life. Beyond fortune telling, gypsies are also believed to possess magic/psychic powers with which they can confer protection against curses, weave spells and bring good luck to people. In this article, we will be focused on gypsy divination.

Here we will explore the different fortune telling methods used by gypsies to educate you on the beliefs and spirituality of the Gypsies.

Gypsy Divination Techniques

To a lot of people, the picture of Gypsy divination is a woman in flowing robes foretelling imminent doom in a poorly lit room with waning candlelight. However, there is much more to Gypsies than that. In several circuses, carnivals and fairs around the world, it wouldn't be out of place to have a different caravan set aside for a Gypsy to harness their psychic powers. People who need to see a Gypsy for divination purposes often go there to have their fortunes read. The Gypsy typically employs a range of fortune reading methods to predict information about your future, and here, we are going to review the common foretelling techniques used by Gypsies in divination.

Dukkering

When it comes to fortune telling, the Gypsies have two words which are used to depict the art. One is "Bocht," a Persian word which means "Sanscritbagya," which can be translated to fate. The second one is "Dukkering," a word derived from a Wallaco-Sclavonian word and is used to refer to something ghostly or something with spiritual connections.

In Gypsy fortune telling, the seers would use playing cards to predict the future/unknown events of an individual. This act of fortune telling by consulting or utilizing a deck of cards is known as Cartomancy. Cartomancy is a widely popular divinatory practice in several cultures across the globe, and it is often considered to be the second most common fortune telling method, after astrology. It is believed that the Gypsies use their psychic powers to read the strange symbolic language of the cards which provides them with a deeper insight to understand people's fortunes and other hidden matters.

The Tarot

Arguably the most popular type of mystical divination involving Cartomancy is the Tarot.

Tarot cards are an ancient set of playing cards used in prophecy to find answers to hidden events and future occurrences. The customary tarot deck is made up of 78 cards. These are 22 Major Arcana cards and 56 Minor Arcana cards. There are however several tarot decks in the market, the three most widely used and known decks being the Rider-Waite, Thoth, and Marseilles.

Now, about tarot readings. Tarot readings are essentially interpretations of a Tarot spread. The spread uses 21 cards, lay out in 7 vertical columns each made up of 3 cards. It is essential to understand each Gypsy may have a different approach or style to tarot reading and as such, two readers may interpret or explain a Gypsy tarot spread in two different ways. The tarot cards are spread from right to left, and when the card must have been spread out as explained above (21 cards in 3 horizontal rows and seven vertical columns), the Gypsy will then read the spread column by column from top to bottom.

While it is a form of fortune telling, the Gypsy Tarot Spread does not just look into the future alone. It also provides insight into past events and the unknown aspects of the present. Typically, the first row represents the past. The second one depicts the present events while the third and last row will be interpreted to tell the future. However, again, the timings of the spread are dependent on the style of the reader.

The Columns

The first column represents the present querent's state of mind. Your thoughts and whatever emotions are you processing now.

The second column gives an overview of your social life and relationships.

The third column depicts the obstacles the querents will face in their journey to achieving their goals in life.

The fourth column shows the querent's expectations, hopes, and ideas in development.

The fifth column brings to light the concealed factors that could influence your fortune. This is where factors like fate and Karma come to play.

The six-column represents the possible happenings in the immediate future of the querent's life. Usually, things that may happen within weeks or in a few months.

The seventh and final column depict the more long term possibilities, things the querent can expect to happen several years down the line.

Tarot readings are also in 2 types; open readings and question readings. Open readings give a general impression of the querent's life while question readings address a specific question asked by the querent.

There is of course, so much more to tarot reading, but for now, I'm only covering the basics. Here is an example of a standard 21 card spread as well as other simple spreads.

21 Card Spread

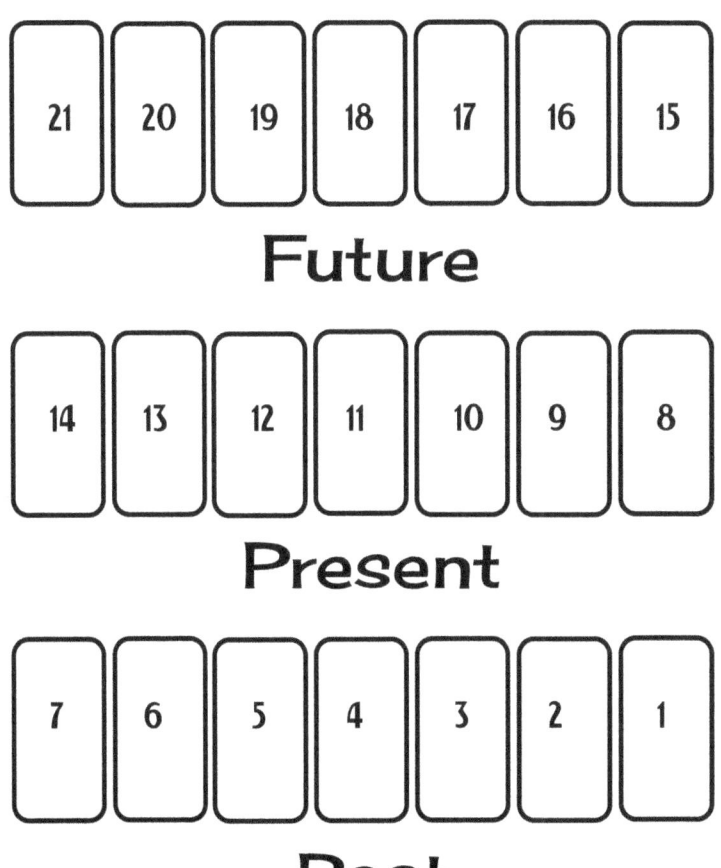

9 Card Spread

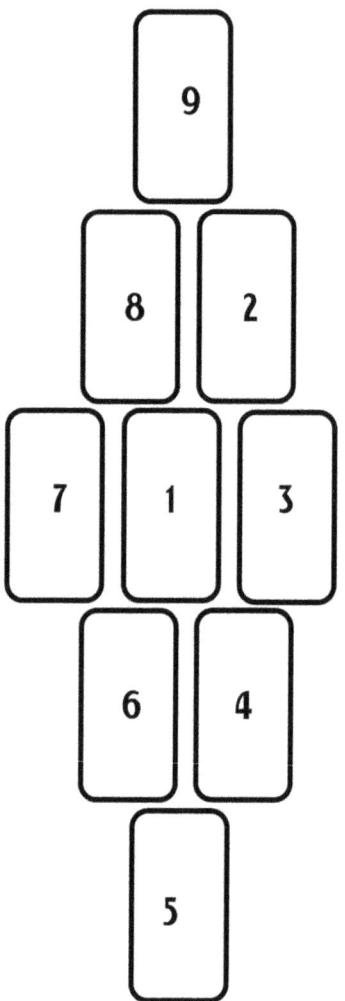

Use this spread to determine the Querent's spiritual direction.

Card 1—The Self Summary.
Card 2—Dreams / Goals.
Card 3—Ideals / Dreams.
Card 4—Practical accomplishments at this moment.
Card 5—Dependencies / False Beliefs.
Card 6—Strengths and positive qualities.
Card 7—Flaws / Weaknesses.
Card 8—Self-image.
Card 9—Wants.

Read card 1 against 2, 4, 6 to get a summary of how things are.
Read card 1 against 3, 8, 9 to evaluate potential.
Read card 1 against 5, 7 to reveal obstacles and areas that require further work.

Universal 3 Card Spread

1	**2**	**3**

Card 1	**Card 2**	**Card 3**
Past	Present	Future
Present Situation	Challenges	Guidance
You	Your Partner	Your Relationship

Making Decisions Spread

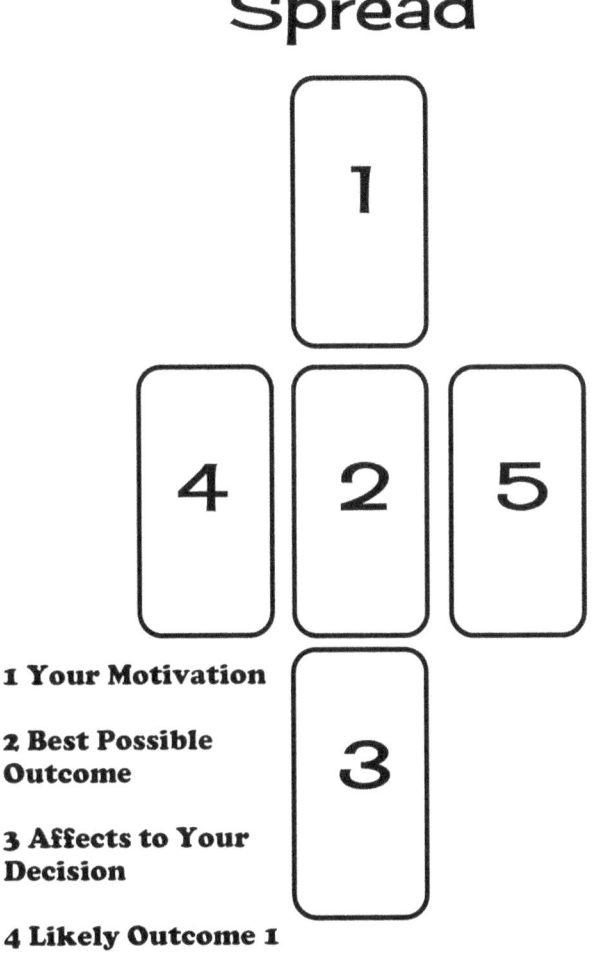

1 Your Motivation

2 Best Possible Outcome

3 Affects to Your Decision

4 Likely Outcome 1

5 Likely Outcome 2

Mirror Spread

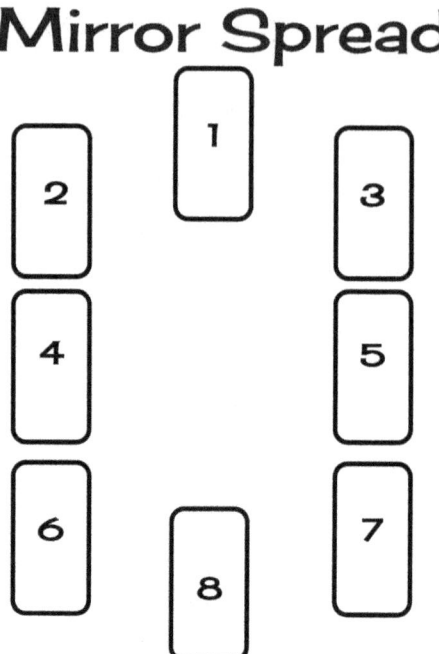

This layout helps an individual evaluate their relationship.

Card 1 indicates the querent.

Card 2 indicates the other person in the relationship.

Card 3 indicates how the querent sees themselves.

Card 4 indicates what the other person's intention towards to the querent.

Card 5 indicates what the querent means to the other person.

Card 6 indicates the obstacles in the relationship,

Card 7 indicates the strengths of the relationship.

Card 8 indicates what the querent's relationship result will be.

The Ellipse Spread

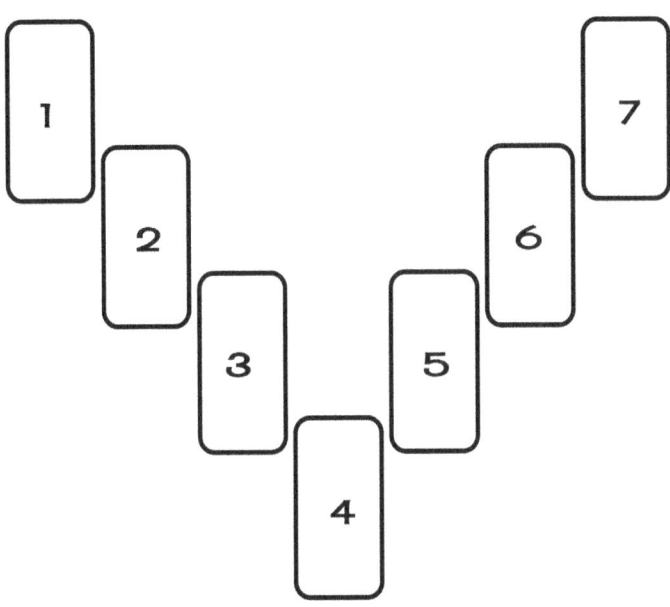

If the querent needs to learn what the result of a project.

Card 1 indicates the past.

Card 2 indicates the present.

Card 3 indicates the future.

Card 4 what solution you have at your disposal.

Card 5 what harm you can come to.

Card 6 what are the hopes and fears associated.

Card 7 what is the outcome of the problem.

Palmistry

Palmistry or palm reading as it is more popularly known as today is the art of foretelling ones future by studying the palm of the querent, taking into consideration palmar features such as the lines on the palms, its texture, and shape including the length and spirals of the fingers. People who read palms are generally referred to as hand readers, palmists or chirologists.

Like the tarot, palmistry is quite a common practice today, and like most other esoteric practices, there are slight cultural variations from place to place. These variations often result in different and sometimes contradicting interpretations of palm readings.

Now, about the technique of palm reading. In palmistry, the lines on the palms are classified under two types; the major lines and the minor lines. The major lines are usually very deep and long; there are 3 in number namely:

The heart line - it is also known as the love or mensal line. The line runs horizontally across the upper part of your palm. It depicts how you handle your emotions and the affairs of your romantic life.

The head line also identified as the wisdom line. It is the middle line, between the heart line and the lifeline. It represents your psychological makeup, intuition, reasoning, intellect and all things mental.

The lifeline - this line starts somewhere between the index finger and the thumb, then it curves downwards and runs down towards the bottom of the palm, terminating at the center of the wrist. The lifeline is considered a pretty big deal in palmistry as it represents your health and how your life will turn out.

The minor lines, sometimes called secondary lines, unlike the major lines are typically fainter and shorter. These lines reveal information about your relationships, influencing factors in your life, your strengths, weaknesses, interests, and talents. The secondary lines include; the fate line, fame line, relationship lines, simian line, children lines, intuition line, health lines, travel line, the girdle of Venus, ring of Apollo, ring of Saturn, ring of Jupiter and bracelets.

In palmistry, the length of the lines (short or long), the consistency (broken or straight), the texture of the lines (deep or faint), the placement, and several other factors are taken into consideration by the palm reader. Sometimes, it may be difficult to place the very faint minor lines on your palms; in some cases they may be absent. Regardless, it is up to the palmist to decipher the meaning of the lines, even the absent ones and gives interpretations as to what it means for the querent.

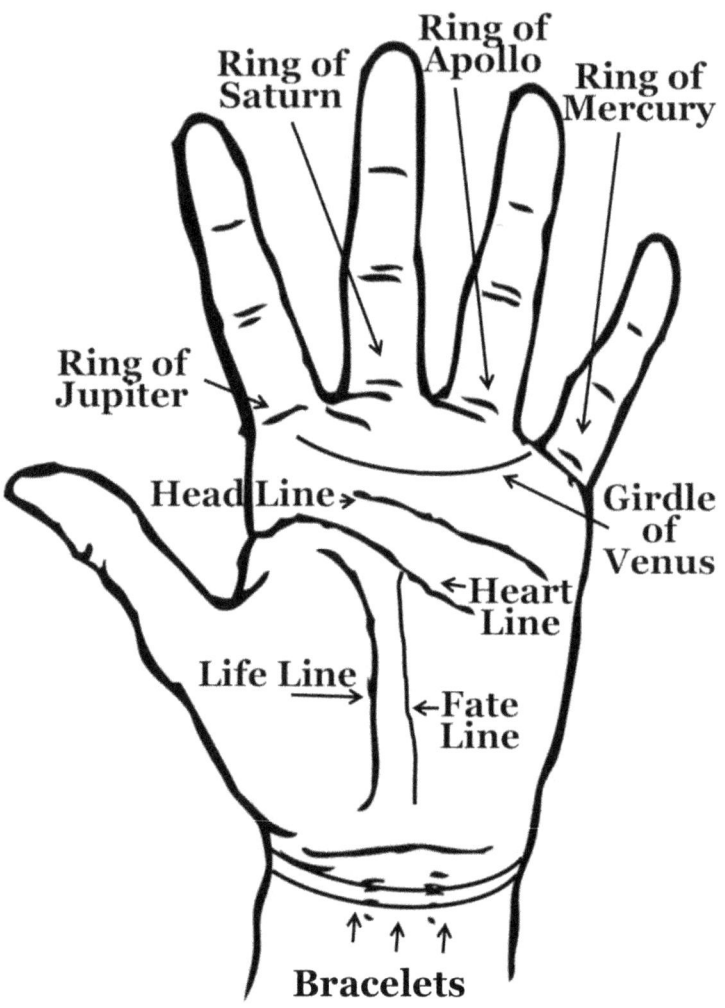

Reading Tea Leaves

The phrase "reading tea leaves" was derived from the term tasseomancy, which is the divination practice of telling someone's fortune by "reading" patterns formed by substances usually tea leaves and coffee grounds. Primarily, here, the foretelling is done by looking at and interpreting the tea leaves in the bottom of a cup. The art of reading tea leaves dates back to the middle ages, hundreds of years ago and although the tea leaves commonly used in the magic practice are in the far East, coffee is also fast becoming the material of choice especially in the Western world.

In this Gypsy divination technique, usually, what happens is that the querent is given a cup of tea or coffee to drink. The querent is expected to drink the liquid leaving just a tiny amount of tea in the bottom of the cup. The cup will be moved around a bit then turned downwards for the remaining liquid to drain out. In this process, some of the tea leaves will get stuck to the bottom of the empty cup while some others will cling to the sides of the cup. The soggy tea usually forms the outline of an image or shapes which are then deciphered and interpreted by the psychic or seer doing the reading.

Like the tarot and palmistry, the process of reading tea leaves varies from one psychic to the other. The wish or question of the querent could also influence the interpretation of the seer while deciphering the meaning behind each symbol. Nevertheless, there are general guidelines for interpreting the meaning of each imagery or shape assumed by the tea leaves. For example, if the substance is shaped like an aircraft, then chances are you may be unsuccessful at any project you have at hand. If it forms cow, castle or trees, then you can expect prosperity and good fortune. A weighing scale means you should anticipate a lawsuit in the future while the hourglass shows that you could be in danger, an imminent one as at that.

Tasseomancy

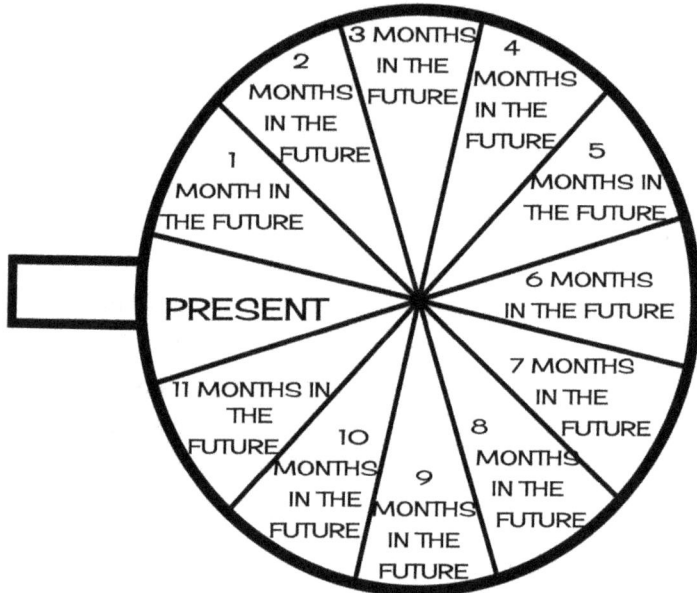

Tasseomancy Symbols and Meanings

- **()** Prosperity and fortune.
- **C** Sleep, rationality, adaptation
- **∩** Bringing together, sum, whole, net.
- **Ɛ** Letter E, bird, exit
- **3** Three
- **ᵜ** Bird, Fire, Mountain
- **ω** Clouds, water.
- **☆** A fortunate sign; if encircled by dots predicts extraordinary wealth and honors. Good luck.
- **♥** Pleasures to come; if followed by a ring, will come by marriage, home; if surrounded by dots, will come through money.
- **⫽** Symbolize journeys and their direction, read in combination with additional signs of travel; wavy lines indicate challenging routes or losses within.
- **†** The cross, a warning of trouble, obstacle or even death.
- **✗** Letter X, Caution, a warning, stop.
- **⚓** A lucky sign; success in business and loyalty in love; if cloudy, the reverse is read.
- **∞** An immediate marriage; if broken, bickering coming.
- **🌀** Energy, creativity, problem-solving.
- **↑** Correct direction, yes.
- **↓** Moving the wrong way, no.
- **=** Steady sailing, no change.
- **⊕** Inheritance is about to fall in. Inevitable change, progress.
- **☉** New Beginnings, Sun, power, energy, success.
- **♀** Pleasure and happiness; if followed by dots, kids or wealth. Many women designate scandal.
- **♂** A male caller visiting. If the arm is held out, he's carrying a gift.

Crystallomancy

Crystallomancy or crystal ball gazing is possibly the most popular form of divination. Any crystal on which the seer is focused correctly can be used for foretelling, and it doesn't have to be in the shape of a ball. For the sake of argument, I'm going to discuss mainly spherical crystal balls. Through the action of crystal-gazing, the seer may perceive images or forms which are believed to give answers to questions that the querent or seer has.

In standard practice, a crystal ball is most frequently utilized. The size of ball favored ranges considerably with those who study crystallomancy. Some crystal ball gazers use a ball which is a few inches in diameter that is held in the palm of the hand. Others prefer a larger crystal ball that sits on a stand or display.

Crystal Ball Selection and Maintenance

Most proficient suggest obtaining your crystal ball in person. You can do one or the other of the next step. Keep your crystal ball in sunlight. Let it soak up the Sun's rays. Afterward, keep your crystal ball displayed on your altar, table, etc. to dissipate the energy of the crystal in every part of the room. The second method is to allow your ball to soak overnight the rays of moonlight especially during the phase of a full moon. When your crystal ball is not in use, it should be covered preferably with black cloth and put away.

A majority of people will notice a haze or cloud of color; on the other hand, others will see a symbol or even a full scenario play out. Your perceptions will vary depending on the practice, feeling and time of day.

Clairvoyants, conjurers, and believers of crystallomancy maintain that crystal gazing produces visionary occurrences and uncanny awareness which allows the seer to look into not just the future, but the past and present as well.

To Start

Crystal ball gazing is best performed on the night of a full moon. Go inside a dark and quiet area.

So you can see, light two candles. The candles will also help by casting back images in the crystal ball.

Burn your favorite incense to get you in the correct mindset. If you feel the need to, add a bit of calming music will do too.

Center yourself by looking into the ball, being mindful not to stare.

Breathe deeply for 15 minutes.

Working the Crystal Ball

With the crystal ball set on a platform in front of you, sit down and relax.

Lay your palms lightly on the ball for 2 minutes to infuse it with your energy.

Reflect on the goal of your scrying session. Visualize your question or express it out loud.

Take your hands off the crystal.

Looking deep into the crystal, allow your eyes to relax and become unfocused.

When you notice smoke emerging in the crystal, allow it to take up the entire ball till you start looking for a picture materializing.

When you are beginning crystal ball gazing, the forms possibly will not make sense to you at first since your mind is still not able to understand what the imagery indicates, you may not see images at all, or it may not even be related to what you desire.

But the longer you work with a crystal ball, the better you will become at it.

The Meanings of Cloud Colors

Blue clouds signify the success of job, career or business.

Gold clouds signify a steady cash flow, prosperity, and revived romance.

Gray/Dark grey clouds signify ill fortune.

Black clouds mean some severely severe stuff is coming one's way.

Green clouds signify health, the happiness of the soul.

Orange clouds signify hidden hostility and anger, troubled emotions.

Red clouds mean a danger to come. This person needs to watch themselves.

Silver clouds signify difficult times ahead accompanied by goodness.

White clouds mean a great fortune to appear.

Yellow clouds signify forthcoming obstructions.

The Closing

To close the crystal gazing session, gradually release the images to fade progressively back into the crystal until it goes back to its initial state.

Thank your crystal ball and smudge or perform a cleansing spell on it before you place it back in storage. A crystal ball is best kept by covering a velvet cloth around it to keep the powers contained.

Remember, you are inviting the forces from the spiritual realm when doing any form of scrying or divination. Unless disturbed, these forces are typically sealed off from this plane. Whenever you perform divination, these forces can serve you, hurt you, or drain you. Using your crystal ball, they can walk through into this world. These consequences are why it is always best to perform a cleansing ritual and a protection ritual beforehand.

Domino Fortune Telling

You might be used to playing a familiar pastime of dominoes with your friends and family, still you might be unfamiliar that you can easily apply them to help foretell what lies ahead.

Gypsies are reported to practice this ancient technique of fortune-telling and divination with a standard Double-Six set.

Primarily with all divination systems, the individual conducting the reading should use their own feeling and intuition to render a more precise definition in the domino tiles, and simply use the meanings represented here as a broad guide. The clairvoyant sense intuition and concentrate them on more specific aspects of their fortune-telling.

The querent should shuffle the dominoes with them all facing down while quietly asking in their mind a question that they want to seek direction on, or merely reflecting their potential future life result.

Each domino tile should be placed and view horizontally. The two faces on each end of a tile are read from left to right.

As a result, the general interpretations of the individual tiles are as follows:

Blank - Blank: Everything is going wrong. This will harm all your activities.

Blank - One: The new beginning of great personal significance is started. This is a moment to be conscious and to make sure that the path you are heading in is what you truly want.

Blank - Two: You will travel and meet new friends. Opportunity for new partnerships and new friendships could be near. But someone could cause difficulties for you.

Blank - Three: Sudden change in romance and love life. You are given a chance for deep integration of the whole self. Take this opportunity now.

Blank - Four: Personal reward beckons. This is a moment for balance. Even if you believed that you and life are already aligned, it's not.

Blank - Five: Substantial change in a professional path. This is a time for the family. It is likewise the perfect time to begin a family such as a family gathering.

Blank - Six: This is a moment for improvement at all stages. It is, however, an especially favorable time for growth and development within the real world. Personal good fortune will show up virtually any undertaking.

One - Blank: A visitor or stranger will bring some exciting news that could mean a financial gain or change your life. However, don't be too trusting. Personal happiness and contentment may be threatened.

One - One: This is the well-defined relationship of two people working as one toward a goal. Don't delay making a critical choice. Peace and love are foretold, and a visitor could be connected.

One - Two: A visit from, or a journey with someone close to you will give you good news. You will come to understand your real purpose

One - Three: Romance found either from someone visiting or on a trip or holiday. A business trip will turn out successfully.

One - Four: There is a demand for harmony inside you. The notable difficulty you face demands resolution. Even though the pain and transition may be unpleasant, they are truly worthwhile. Materialistic or monetary gain associated with a journey or trip.

One - Five: Gracefully accept help when it is offered. You have done so much by yourself. Someone will be there to help share this weight with you. A love interest or proposition will steer you on an emotional experience, or you will tend a social function starting you on a journey of development.

One - Six: Too many things have been delayed for too long. Now is the time to complete some of those plans that you have held off on. You will feel so much better when they are completed. A trip, journey, or vacation will probably head to permanent emotional or individual comfort.

Two - Blank: A break is in order. You definitely need some time out from everything.

Two - One: You may find the essentials escaping you around this time; wallet, keys, phone, etc. Financial difficulties and perhaps a loss of money or assets are indicated.

Two - Two: A personal wish will come true, and you will get what you want. Jealousy may occur as enemies try to spoil your own happiness and business success.

Two - Three: This domino signifies a difficulty to the ins and outs of your physical presence. It displays a period of uncertainty and a need for you to focus yourself and discover a clear intention and purpose. A partner will enter or leave however will be extremely close to your social group.

Two-Four: You have the opportunity for advancement. Don't let it pass you by. Learn all you can get so that you have a more excellent knowledge of just what the fact is. Wealth increased, perhaps an inheritance, through a loved one or dear friend.

Two - Five: You are being delivered information from spirit in your dreams. Pay attention and make observations on all your dreams.

Two - Six: You have merely glimpsed the opportunities and grazed at the surface of your personal capability. It is time to reach for and obtain more important spiritual objectives.

Three - Blank: Greed or love of money will lead to extreme difficulty. You possibly will undergo unforeseen obstacles at home and at work.

Three - One: The answer to the question in your mind is no. A bombshell comes to you and those near to you. It's difficult to determine if it's good or bad. Some critical but surprising news is nearing. Strangers may create unhappiness for you.

Three - Two: An outstanding debt will be honored so be careful with your money around this time. Don't start splurging on unnecessary things. Successful changes are coming your way, but you still need to be careful now in your financial affairs.

Three - Three: This domino predicts concerns in your emotional life. If you have felt upset about an issue, know that what you need to know is being made available to you. The time is here to make a choice, and the decision will be evident. Much wealth or an object of high value is strongly favored.

Three - Four: A happy relationship, or a marriage.

Three - Five: There is a wave of anger inside you that needs to be released. You've held your tongue long enough, and it is doing you more harm than good.

Three - Six: You may be lucky in love, but it could be problematic and challenging.

Four - Blank: A love interest may turn out to be unsatisfying, or Bad news is on its progress. A message of some sorts might back you up. Do your best to not to let it overwhelm you or resolve a dispute.

Four - One: Debts loom, leading to trouble financial problems lie ahead. Pay any outstanding debts now to avoid problems in the future. Some money worry may be on the future so begin planning in advance.

Four - Two: There are setbacks indicated. You may encounter losses directly or monetarily valuable from being misplaced or even from theft.

Four - Three: You may have forgotten your way a little bit amidst some turmoil at home. Time to move on with the spiritual work that has been taking second place in your life while you have been taking care of the physical aspect. It will soon pass.

Four - Four: Happiness, joy, and pleasure. Now is the moment to let loose. You may receive an invite to a prosperous and lively event. This is an opportunity to think for you. Not the time to play it safe.

Four - Five: Don't be hasty with your decisions. Every decision you make affects others as well as you. Think twice before you act.

Four - Six: Unexpected change in your prosperity, status, or general fortune. Karma is in full effect. The energies that you have sent into the Universe will now return to you by the equivalent intent with which they were initially sent.

Five - Blank: There will be some sadness. Someone near you is about to get serious news. You will have to give support but be very cautious regarding anything you decide to say.

Five - One: A brand-new spark is ignited. You will shortly chance upon a new love interest or a new friend. Either a new romantic partner will quickly enter your life, or you will reawaken the fire in your existing relationship. But step mindfully, or else things may end unfortunately for those in love. There may be a chance for passionate romance, possibly through work.

Five - Two: A shift in career, position, or wage for either you, a relative or someone close which will have an effect on your way of life.

Five - Three: Your boss or someone from your past may give some critical news or helpful advice. It isn't clear if it is good or bad.

Five - Four: Look for a raise or a career move for the better. Invest now, and your benefits will be generous. Good fortune waits in the nearby future. Take the risk.

Five - Five: Changes are developing your way. It's time to see things from a new outlook. A change to your home or a new one may be helpful to you where you will be happy. There will be a chance for you to obtain money from a new approach.

Five - Six: This is the reward for following a correct path. You may find success at work, in your career, or possibly a form of education. All the difficulties and struggles are over.

Six - Blank: You may notice you don't really know someone as well as you thought you did. Be mindful of deceitful friends or a deceptive person. You could go through a considerable dilemma, or a rumor may be approaching.

Six - One: A close friend or family member will need you for help or advice shortly. Do your best to help them. There will be an end to your problems. A good friend will help you overcome your obstacles. A wedding is foretold.

Six - Two: Material possessions may come into your hands which you might not know what to do with at first. Good fortune in career, work, or a personal financial opportunity. Good luck is moving your way, and your position will progress.

Six - Three: A trip or a journey is in your future that will influence your life.

Six - Four: Conflict may be on the prospect. This may have to do with money or a legal issue. All the signals point to a dispute, perhaps even an action, with an ineffective result.

Six - Five: Help arising from a dear friend or colleague, but, you will still require persistence and determination to succeed. A kind of action will bring you high regard. A significant event is in the offing so prepare as best you can

Six - Six: A really favorable draw. This draw predicts luck, success, and fortune in every aspect of your life.

Reading the Dominoes

There are many arrangements for reading dominoes. Here are a few you may want to try.

Past, Present, and Future Reading Method 1

Spread all the dominoes facing down and mix-up them fully. Pull three tiles out.

Past, Present, and Future Reading Method 2

Spread all the dominoes facing down and mix-up them completely. Draw one tile out and place aside. Reshuffle the remaining tiles. Pick another tile out and put aside. Shuffle. Pull the last tile.

Three Tile Shuffle

Spread out all the dominoes facing down shuffling them entirely. Pull one tile out and then placed back into the remaining tiles. Reshuffle the tiles. Pull another tile out and then put back into the rest of the tiles. Reshuffle and draw the last tile. This approach may produce a tile being picked two or yet three times. In the event this happens then, the reading will appear very immediately.

The Celtic Cross

Based on the Tarot reading, the Celtic Cross is a design used to fortune tells with dominoes. The querent pulls one at a time, ten tiles from the shuffled tiles. These tiles are then set in front of the clairvoyant. In order, the clairvoyant takes the tiles and arranges them. Be careful not to alter the orientation of the dominoes.

The Past, Present, and Future Reading

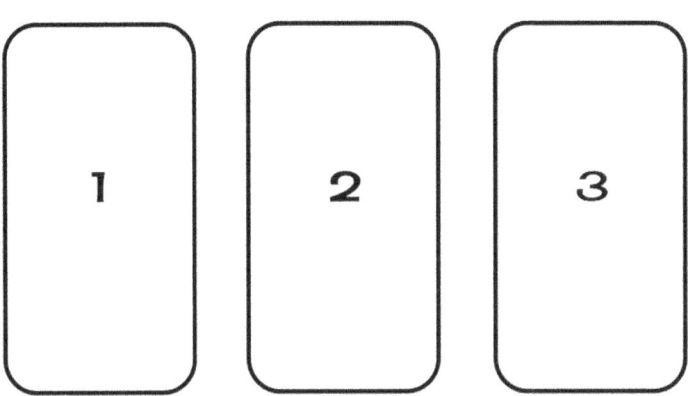

1 - The querent's recent past.
2 - What issue is the querent facing right now?
3 - The querent's immediate future.

The Celtic Cross

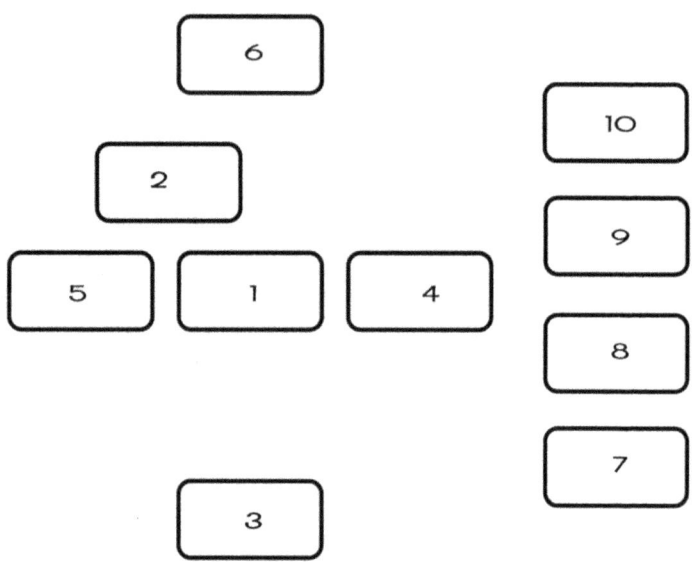

1 - The problem or predicament of the querent.
2 - What issue is the querent facing right now?
3 - The querent's immediate history.
4 - The querent's recent past.
5 - The querent's immediate future.
6 - The querent's intention, aim, or objective.
7 - The querent's personal emotions.
8 - Connections to the querent's external forces.
9 - The querent's wants, desires, and concerns.
10 - The final result for the querent.

Dreams

Dreams can sometimes be used to interpret the future. This divination practice is known as oneiromancy. It is believed that dreams can provide insights into what the future holds for an individual. Dreams are a universal phenomenon, everyone dreams and whether or not we remember our dreams when we wake up does not invalidate the fact that everyone does in fact dream.

Owing to the universality of dreams, it is not unsurprising that oneiromancy is one of the oldest forms of divination.

It is believed that dreams can provide us with wisdom and guidance to navigate the affairs of our life. However, dreams are not always as straightforward as one would expect. They are often coded, and you may need a seer or psychic to interpret the dreams for you.

Here are just a few examples:

Losing Your Teeth

Teeth falling out are typical dream symbols. It just means you're frightened or worried about the transformations going on in your life now. Causing you to lose faith and in your ability to deal with it. This may mark a fear of growing old and being unattractive to others.

Being Pursued

Being chased by something or someone is usually brought about by a specific event or a particular person. Sometimes it's the feeling of you being pursued, and so you run and keep running. You are evading obstacles in your life instead of addressing them. Possibly, your subconscious is trying to send you the information that you need to solve the problem.

Naked In Public

Dreaming of being naked means there is a situation that makes you feel vulnerable and exposed. When you are entering a position that is new to you, feeling a lack of confidence in your abilities, you will usually experience this dream.

Flying

The flying idea reflects that you have managed to create an opportunity for yourself. Also the feeling of freedom and shows you have been released from some limitation or circumstances that were crushing on you. This has a tendency to happen when we are feeling empowered when things are really looking up.

Jumping High

Oftentimes if we jump very high in our dreams, it actually turns into a flying dream. The fact is the most straightforward means of flying in your dreams is only to jump so high and notice what follows.

If you're just jumping remarkably high however not flying, it can suggest you desire more independence in life, although you believe you're being held back by someone or something.

Falling

These dreams imply stress and a lack of control in your conscious life. This is a sign something in your world is spinning out of control. You feel you will be crashing after succeeding. This dream occurs the most often out of all the dreams.

The Dead

Dreaming about a deceased relative or still just seeing the person is a way of your mind only receiving closure. If you dream of someone who has died a long ago, then it may imply that a current relationship or circumstance in your life resembles the quality of that deceased person. On the other hand, it may also be a way for you to resolve your feelings with those who have passed on.

Going Abroad

If you dream of going abroad, it could mean that you may meet an influential new friend soon enough.

A Disaster

To dream of a disaster is instead surprisingly interpreted to be a forerunner of good things to come in your life.

Echoes

If you hear an echo in your dreams, then the good news is imminent.

In Jail

A dream of you in jail is a warning against obstacles that may hinder your progress in life.

Remember

Foretelling is by no means a modern practice. In the middle ages, Gypsies were usually consulted by royalties to see and tell what the future had in store for the kingdom. Kings often got inspirations from the foretelling to make important decisions such as making treaties and going into battles. Since those times, Gypsy divination has only become more prevalent in pop culture, and from the look of things, foretelling will keep breathing even in future generations. It is essential to understand that Gypsy divination does not have the power to change future events. However, it can help you anticipate them, get you psyched for life's possibilities and maybe even avoid the pitfalls.

5
AMULETS, CHARMS, AND TALISMANS

In gypsy lore, when the Romani call upon magic, it's generally using amulets, or talismans to enhance their charms. This is something which is a part of their lifestyle. The current generation cherishes a belief that is passed down from generation to generation and as such. To the Romani, there is a secure connection between magic and nature, just as it is in other magical cultures.

Amulets

An amulet, in gypsy lore, is an item from nature that is charged, either naturally, or through ritual, with magical power. A typical amulet would be a stone with a hole through it, known as a Hag stone or a Four Leaf Clover.

Some people make the mistake of purchasing or obtaining a good luck charm just to put it aside and forget it. Your amulet should remain close. Keep it in your handbag or pocket, or worn around your neck. It is a living thing, and it should be touched frequently, with a perception of happiness and hope.

The more you believe an amulet will work, the more useful it will be. If you view your charm or good luck item with doubt, thinking, "I am never lucky." "This will never work." Guess what? It won't.

Talismans

Talismans are human-made objects charged with magical energy by the gypsy sorcerer. A common talisman would be a piece of parchment, wood or a coin, with particular words of power or symbols written on it.

Charms

The most widely used charms are: Black stones, Jade, Seashells, Sharks Tooth, Tiger's Eye stone, White stones and more.

Putsi it All Together

Putsi bags are a type of magical bag or pouch used in the Romanichal culture to provide protection; cast spells, or gives blessings. They, in reality, serve as hex bags or gris-gris bags. Shamans also use pouches such as these, but call them Medicine Bags, and they will generally carry herbs for medicinal purposes. A putsi bag will hold herbs, bones, many other ingredients, including an item about the designated victim or person in need of protection.

These bags can be carried on you, hung from your review mirror (I have one to protect my car), tucked under a bed pillow, etc. Putsi bags should have an odd number of objects higher than one inside including a charm, talisman or amulet inside representing its desired outcome.

Every practitioner has their own process of preparing a putsi bag. There are specific steps in the process that are recognized to be universal. The steps for creating a putsi bag is usually performed on an altar or other sacred place and will often be accompanied by the burning of candles and incense.

Before creating your putsi bag, select a cloth bag whose color echoes with your intention. Here is a brief list to help you determine the most suitable color for your putsi bag.

Red - Represents energy, excitement, power, passion, protection, overcomes fear, and strength.

Pink - Represents spiritual love, romance, success, attraction, compassion, understanding, gentleness, friendship, forgiveness, self-respect, mends broken hearts, and overcomes conflict.

Orange - Can be substituted for Gold. Used for success, emotional clarity, control, happiness, pleasure, attracts luck and money, passion, energy, hopefulness, and confidence.

Yellow - Represents attraction, success, drawing, communicating, studying, memory, clear thinking, decision making, and confidence.

Green - Represents fertility, better business, creative ideas, money, employment, rewards, good luck, earth, plants, and growth.

Blue - Represents harmony, loyalty, astral travel, and tranquility. For psychic ability, integrity, truth, meditation, kindness, knowledge, diminishes excess energy, decreases anxiety and stress, helps insomnia.

Purple - Consisting of blue and red energy. Represents competition, achieve work success, wealth, dignity, overcome odds, court cases, awareness, victory, fights negativity.

White - All-purpose spiritual awareness and power. Purity, truth, spiritual devotion, cooperation, assistance

Gold - The Sun. success, wealth, wishes, happiness

Silver - Gray is often used for silver. Use for quick money, gambling, moon magick

Gray - Neutralizes Stress, Negativity, Decreases the Impact of Mistakes, Cleanse Energies, and Exorcisms

Black - Freedom from Evil, Transformation

Brown - Consistency, Fertility, Thrift, Work, Awareness, Control, Fruitful, Success in Business, Grounding, Long-Term Accomplishments, Growth, Resolution, Planting

After you have chosen the proper bag color, you must activate it. Start by scoring a candle with your intention. Using nine pins, Pierce the candle affirming your request with the impaling of each pin. The last pin should be inserted precisely through the wick of the candle. Light the appropriate incense before lighting your candle.

What you put in your putsi bag is as important as the color of the bag. Fill the bag with the equivalent stones, herbs, and symbols of your intention.

Here are some ways you can create your own:

For Love

Objects to Use:

Acorn, Bell, Bird Egg, Gold Ring, Keys, Mirror, Orange Zest, Owl Feather, Pea Pod, Pink or Red Silk Thread with Three Knots, Pink or Red Silk, Small Horseshoe, Snake Eggs, Tea Leaves, Walnut Shells,

Stones to Use:

Aquamarine, Black Opal, Cat's Eye, Diamond, Garnet, Heliotrope, Lapis Lazuli, Moonstone, Onyx, Opal, Pearls, Rose Quartz, Ruby, Sardonyx

Plants and Herbs to Use:

Basil, Bay Leaf , Betony, Caraway, Cardamom, Catnip, Chamomile, Cinnamon, Cinquefoil, Coriander, Couch Grass Root, Fennel, Gentian, Ginseng, Hawthorn Berries, Hibiscus, Jasmine, Juniper, Lavender, Lemon Mint, Linden, Lovage, Maidenhair Grass, Mallow, Mandrake, Marjoram, Mistletoe, Peppermint, Periwinkle, Poppy, Primrose, Rose, Rosemary, Saffron, Skullcap, Thyme, Valerian, Vervain, Violet, Wild Strawberry, Wormwood, Yarrow.

For Health

Objects to Use:

Acorn, Buckeye, Coral, Eel Skin, Fox Fur, Gold Coin, Horseshoe Nail, Red Flannel, Snake Skin, Walnut, White Stone, Wool

Stones to be Use:

Agate, Amber, Amethyst, Beryl, Chalcedony, Diamond, Emerald, Garnet, Jade, Jasper, Lapis Lazuli, Magnetite, Malachite, Moonstone, Opal, Pearls, Quartz, Rose Ruby, Sapphire, Sardonyx, Topaz, Turquoise, Zircon.

Plants and Herbs to Use:

Angelica, Camphor, Cloves, Coriander, Cornflower, Fennel, Groundsel, Juniper, Marjoram, Mullein, Nutmeg, Parsley, Plantain, Rosemary, Rue, Sage, St. John's Wort, Thyme, Wormwood

For Protection from Evil Eye

Objects to Use:

Acorns, Ash, Coral, Iron, Lemon Peel, a Mirror, Nail of a Horseshoe, Pewter, Salt, Urine

Stones to Use:

Alexandrite, Amethyst, Beryl, Black Tourmaline, Carnelian, Cat's Eye, Emerald, Garnet, Jade, Jasper, Jet, Malachite, Moonstone, Onyx, Opal, Quartz, Sapphire, Sardonyx, Topaz, Turquoise

Plants and Herbs to Use:

Aloe, Angelica, Anise, Apple, Basil, Buckthorn, Burdock, Cinnamon, Cinquefoil, Cumin, Dill, Fennel, Garlic, Hazel, Heather, Heliotrope, Hyacinth, Hyssop, Juniper, Lavender, Lemon, Lime, Milk Thistle, Myrrh, Nettle, Nightshade, Parsley, Pennyroyal, Sage, St. John's Wort, Valerian, Violet, Wormwood

For Power and Strength

Objects to Use:

Acorn, Black Stone, Coral, Flint, Gold Coin, Horseshoe Nail, Iron, Oak Chip, Tooth or Animal Claw

Stones to Use:

Alexandrite, Amazonite, Beryl, Beryl, Bloodstone, Diamond, Emerald, Garnet, Jade, Moonstone, Opal, Quartz, Rock Crystal, Topaz, Zircon

Plants and Herbs to Use:

Borage, Cinnamon, Cloves, Gentian, Honeysuckle, Linen, Mandrake Root, Moss, Mugwort, Nutmeg, Rosemary, Rowan, Sage, Thyme, Verbena

For Prosperity

Object To Use:

Acorn, Almonds, Coral, Dice, Glass Beads, Gold Coin, Magnet, Magnifying Glass, Silver Coin

Stones to Use:

Black Opal, Diamond, Emerald, Green Tourmaline, Moonstone, Quartz, Ruby, Turquoise

Plants and Herbs to Use:

Alfalfa, Apple, Basil, Chamomile, Cinnamon, Cinquefoil, Clover, Cloves, Comfrey, Dill, Elderberry, Fenugreek, Flax, Ginger, Honeysuckle, Iris, Jasmine, Marjoram, Mint, Myrtle, Patchouli, Periwinkle, Pine Nuts, Poppy, Sesame, Sorrel, Verbena.

6
SIMPLE SPELLS

Gypsies have been notable charmers and fortunetellers of the magical arts, and they have undoubtedly had an intense influence on the development of folk magic

The folklore of these spiritual travelers of the world is abounding with incantations and superstitions.

Gypsy folk magic relies heavily upon the application of herbs, seashells, eggs, and other natural amulets, as well as human hair. Many Gypsy spells for the fulfillment of love or the warding off of the evil eye.

To Get More Attention from Your Partner

Relax before a dying fire and gaze into it, freeing your mind of all but thoughts of your partner.

Set a small bin of laurel leaves between your knees.

Holding your gaze locked on the fire, drop your dominant hand into the basket; pick out a handful of leaves. Toss them onto the fire. As they burst into flames, recite out loud the following:

"Laurel leaves that burn in the fire,

Draw unto me my heart's desire."

Wait until the fires have died down, and repeat the process. Do this a total of three times.

Within a day, your partner will call on you.

To Dream of the One You Will Marry

When you rise in the morning, peel a small lemon. Retain two even parts of the peel, each approximately the dimension of a half-dollar. Arrange the pieces with the peel side out, and the insides are touching each other. Put them in your bag or your right-hand pocket, if that's your dominant side. Leave them there the whole day.

At night, when you get undressed for bed, remove the peel from your pocket or bag and rub the legs of the bed with it. Place both pieces of the skin under your pillow and go to sleep.

If you dream of your love, you will undoubtedly marry him or her.

Attracting a Specific Lover

Set a wineglass on the table. Suspend a ring from a piece of red silk ribbon.

Keeping the ribbon between your thumb and forefinger, with your elbow relaxing on the table, allow the ring dangle in the rim of the wineglass like a pendulum. Try to hold the ring still.

In a powerful, clear voice, state your name following that, the name of your hopeful love. Recite the name of your love three times in all.

Then, spelling his or her name out, allow the ring to swing until it strikes on the side of the wineglass. You'll get one clink for each letter.

Take the ribbon and fasten it around your neck, letting the ring to drape down on your chest over your heart. You will carry it for three weeks.

Each Friday, repeat the preceding ritual. By the close of the third week, if it is meant to be, then the loved one will come to you.

To Have an Item Returned

Set an iron nail on a window ledge. In whichever direction the person who has the object lives, the nail should point.

Now, will the item back each time you see the nail, by focusing on it. When the item has been returned the nail should be buried or returned with others.

Protecting a Child from the Other Side

Secure small amount dirt from any grave, usually a parent, balancing it on the back of the left hand. When the child is leaving and not looking, toss the dirt over their head to provide them protection.

Bless and Protect Your New Home

Plant garlic around the boundary of your home.

Sprinkle salt around the perimeter of your home.

Winning the Lottery

For every numbers to be picked, light one green candle. Sit silently and ponder the flames, giving each flame to suggest a number.

Fill in the game slip according to the numbers that appear into your head. Sprinkle the game slip with nutmeg and then extinguish the candles. Leave the game slip sprinkled with nutmeg for a day before completely sweeping it off.

Iron Healing

Take an iron nail or if you have one, a horseshoe to bless it by soaking it in salty water. Bury it in a potted plant, flower bed or garden of the person who is sick. Leave a tip poking out of the dirt, to serve as a conduit to scatter the energy.

When you bury it, say:

Ill health I now tell,

Run through this iron.

(Name of individual) is free and well.

To Remove a Problem

Write your issue or obstacle on a piece of paper. Digging a hole, place the paper on the inside, and bury it along with a piece of iron, copper and some zinc.

Here's Another One

Write the problem on an old shoe's sole bottom. Get the shoe, step with determination the issue three times, and then takes the shoe and burn it in the fire.

To Discourage an Unwelcomed Visitor

To ward off visits or calls from unwanted people, the only thing you need is salt. Immediately after the unwelcome visitor is gone, sprinkle the salt, which is purifying and protective against the forces of evil, in the soil where the person has stepped on.

Bulb Spell

Using a bulb plant such as tulips, daffodils, hyacinths, crocuses, or even onions, chant the name of your love while planting your preferred bulb in a brand new clean flower pot. Every day in the morning and evening, recite:

While this root grows

And as this flower blows,

May his/her heart be

Directed at me.

As each day passes, the one whom you love will be more and more inclined to you, till you get your heart's desire.

Mandrake Love Amulet

To promote everlasting love between a couple's arousing sexual passions both partners should carry a piece of Mandrake root from the same plant

Love Potion

For women to win over a man, brew the seeds of a female fern. For a man to win over a woman, prepare the seeds of male fern. Give to the person who heart you are trying to capture.

Gypsy Aphrodisiac

To be overcome by lustful urges, take fresh roots of an asparagus plant and boiled in red wine. Drink in place of breakfast, for seven consecutive mornings.

Gypsy Love Spell for Men

If you wish to make a particular woman fall in love with you, secretly take one of her shoes, filling it with rue leaves, hang it over your bed.

7
GYPSY SUPERSTITIONS

Superstitions are an integral part of everyday life for Romanians. They are holding to a belief in charms, amulets, curses, bad luck, and ghosts. Gypsy culture is immersed in superstition. Gypsies observe many rites, and, as happens in many religions, most of their rituals are linked to placating or warding off energies or spirits in an attempt to manipulate destiny. Understanding of them and their recognized influence depends on numerous aspects including region and age.

Learn some of these superstitions. You'll see many of you actually believe in.

A baby born before the Sabbath at midnight will be beneath a curse.

A baby will keep its luck in the dirty lines of its hands.

A crow being in the street implies a pleasant journey.

A dead crow in the street would make a gypsy to turn back.

A moth fluttering about the flame of a candle signifies a letter coming in the morning.

At a funeral, at least one window should always be opened, to allow the spirit to leave.

Breaking a glass will banish bad luck.

Crying at your wedding brings good luck.

Do not bake bread, sow flax or use needle or scissors, on Wednesday or Friday.

If born at a full moon, a baby will be lucky.

To have good luck the rest of the year, wear something new for Easter

If a bearer at a funeral stumbles during the death march, there will be another death.

If a cat washes her face and paws in the hallway, it means guests are coming.

If a dog cries for no reason, anticipate a death.

To hear an owl in the daytime is a bad omen.

Throwing frogspawn over your left shoulder brings good luck.

There will be a quarrel in the future if a wood or coal fire creates any noise.

Spitting on your hand after seeing a wagtail indicates that money is on its way.

Seeing a shooting star is a harbinger of death.

Scratching of the right eye indicates sadness.

Scratching of the left eye is a sign of happiness to come.

You will be giving divine protection when you pitch a tent near a holly tree.

Once you leave the house, never look back or else your entire day will go wrong.

Never close an agreement on Friday.

Newly sprouted grass or of brightening means there will be a burial.

On Mondays, never make payments, or you will give money all week.

Never put your handbag on the floor, or else you will lose money.

Meeting a woman carrying a jug full of water is lucky, but it's unlucky if it is empty.

If your ears are red, it means someone is idly talking about you.

If you were a bridesmaid three times, then you will remain unmarried.

If you notice a mule shaking itself is a sign of good luck.

If you bite your tongue while eating, you recently told a lie.

If your right hand itches, money will be paid out.

If your left hand itches, money will be received.

A priest will visit you if the cat is washing on the threshold.

If smoke clings to the ground, rain is on the way.

Breaking a mirror you will give you seven years of bad luck

Telling a fisherman good luck will provide him with bad luck.

To spin clothes on Thursday is unlucky.

To wash anything on Saturday is unlucky.

If a fire burns bright and steady in spring or autumn, expect a frost.

There is a treasure to be found, where the first swallow is seen.

You will have good luck all day if you see a white horse in the morning.

You will remain single if you sit at the table corner.

Your nose tickling is a sign of you getting drunk.

8
INTERNATIONAL ROMANI DAY

The International Romani Day is not just celebrated but observed on April 8th every year and is more than just a highlight of the Roma culture, but it focuses on the persecution and discrimination faced by the Roma people in Europe in every part of life.

According to genetic studies, the Roma people migrated from modern day Pakistan and India about 1500 years ago to the European continent at the same time. These people lived in groups and spread out throughout Europe throughout history. The Roma people are a minority in Europe, and there are just about 11 million Roma in Europe today.

There are many similarities between the Roma people and the people of Pakistan & India. Even though the Roma people have lived in Europe for centuries, culture and hospitality are similar to the South Asian countries.

Struggle for Their Rights

The Roma people have been harassed and victimized throughout European history with Hitler's Nazis killing a record 200,000 to 1,500,000 Roma. After World War II, the Roma people who lived in the Communist countries were severely persecuted with many even being sterilized to reduce their population in Europe.

The International Romani day is a day when we can raise awareness about the struggles of the Roma people. Even though the Roma are Europe's largest minority group, they have been voiceless for centuries. They have been misrepresented, stereotypes, mythologized, segregated, persecuted and systemically discriminated by the system and general public.

Fight for their Rights

It is during the 1960s that Romani organizations had been established in France and the UK to create international awareness about the group of people and the number of Romani organizations has only continued to grow since then. The first success after many failed attempts had made in 1971 when many European nations met in Orpington near London to discuss the rights of the Romani people.

It is during this international meeting of Roma that the International Romani Union was formed. A Romani flag had been accepted, and a song "Gelem, Gelem" had been composed by the famous Jarko Javonic to become the anthem for the organization. It is the same union which declared 8th April as the International Romani Day.

A Day to Discuss Challenges

On the International Romani Day each year, the challenges and issues faced by the Romani community are discussed, and the Roma people come together to find solutions for their problems. During this day, protection and promotion of human rights are provided to all people.

The Roma people have gone suffered from many hate crimes by the European people, and it is time that European history acknowledged what the Roma people went through. The Roma people had been called Gypsies which is a derogatory term. The Romani culture and history have been mythologized and made fun of by people. International Romani Day is the time of the year when the Romani people from throughout the world and not just Europe come together to celebrate their culture and raise awareness.

GLOSSARY TERMS

Aleuromancy - Divination using flour or meal. For a particular querent, related sentences or messages correlating to the querent's question are written on tiny bits of paper. These little pieces of paper were next rolled up into balls of cornmeal or flour.

These balls are then shifted around nine times and given to the querent who would then pick a ball.

Amulets - An object, either natural or human-made, believed to be imbued with extraordinary abilities to bring good fortune or protect.

Axinomancy - Prediction of the future using the head of an ax or hatchet through reading the orientation of the handle or the quivering of the blade.

Belomancy - An ancient art of divination using arrows. It is also known as bolomancy.

Bibliomancy - Divination using a book, randomly opening to a specific page, a dictionary is suitable for this.

Capnomancy - Interpreting pictures made by smoke. It is also known as libanomancy.

Cartomancy - Divination or fortune-telling using a deck of cards. This is typically performed with Tarot cards.

Catoptromancy - Divination using a mirror. It is also known as enoptromancy.

Charms - A magical spell or an object, such as a lucky coin, that brings luck.

Chiromancy - Foretelling the future through the study of the palm Also known as Palmistry and palm reading.

Chirologists - Individuals who read palms also known as hand readers, or palmists.

Cleromancy - Lot casting, similar to divination using dice, pebbles, colored crystals, beans, small sticks or bones.

Coscinomancy - Divination using a sieve and shears.

Crystallomancy - For seeing visions achieved through trance induction using a crystal ball. It is also known as crystal gazing, crystal-seeing.

Dactylomancy - A form of divination using a suspended ring.

Hydromancy - Divination utilizing water, including the appearance, ebb, and flow, or ripples created by pebbles dropped in a pond, lake, etc.

Kleidoscopy - Divination using keys or chance spoken exchanges.

Lecanomancy - A form of divination interpreting patterns using the mixing oil and water in a bowl or a dish.

Libanomancy - A practice of divination by observing and deciphering burning incense including the way incense ash drop. It is also known as livanomancy and knissomancy.

Lychnoscopy - Divination using candles by reading the forecasts from the movements of the flame.

Metoscopy –Is a form of divination in which the diviner foretells personality, character, and destiny, based on the pattern of lines on the client's forehead.

Oneiromancy - Divination which involving dreams. You are interpreting dreams to predict the future. It is also known as dream reading.

Ooscopy - Divination using eggs by interpreting the shapes from the separated egg white when it is dropped into hot water.

Oracle - D priest or priestess who serves as a medium to give advice or prophesize. They are also known as a seer.

Pendulum - One of the oldest methods of divination consisting of a weight, or bob, which hangs freely from a chain or string.

Psychography - Enabling a person to create written words without knowingly writing. It is also known as automatic writing and spirit writing.

Putsi - A kind of pouch utilized in the Romanichal culture to give blessings, cast spells, or provides protection.

Pyromancy - Divination using fire or flame. Pyromancy is thought to be one of the earliest methods of divination.

Querent - A person who seeks advice.

Rhabdomancy - Dowsing divination method which involves the use of any stick, arrow, rod, wand, staff, etc. It is also known as Rahabdoscopy.

Talismans - Object believed to hold magical properties to bring good luck or protect from evil or harm.

Tasseography - Divination by reading tea leas or coffee grounds.

ABOUT THE AUTHOR

Monique Joiner Siedlak is a writer, witch, and warrior on a mission to awaken people to their greatest potential through the power of storytelling infused with mysticism, modern paganism, and new age spirituality. At the young age of 12, she began rigorously studying the fascinating philosophy of Wicca. By the time she was 20, she was self-initiated into the craft, and hasn't looked back ever since. To this day, she has authored over 40 books pertaining to the magick and mysteries of life.

To find out more about Monique Joiner Siedlak artistically, spiritually, and personally, feel free to visit her **official website**.

www.mojosiedlak.com

facebook.com/mojosiedlak
x.com/mojosiedlak
instagram.com/mojosiedlak
pinterest.com/mojosiedlak
bookbub.com/authors/monique-joiner-siedlak

MORE BOOKS BY MONIQUE

African Spirituality Beliefs and Practices

Hoodoo

Seven African Powers: The Orishas

Cooking for the Orishas

Lucumi: The Ways of Santeria

Voodoo of Louisiana

Haitian Vodou

Orishas of Trinidad

Connecting with your Ancestors

Blood Magick

The Orishas

Vodun: West Africa's Spiritual Life

Marie Laveau: Life of a Voodoo Queen

Candomblé: Dancing for the God

Umbanda

Exploring the Rich and Diverse World

Divination Magic for Beginners

Divination with Runes

Divination with Diloggún

Divination with Osteomancy

Divination with the Tarot

Divination with Stones

The Beginner's Guide to Inner Growth

Astral Projection for Beginners

Meditation for Beginners

Reiki for Beginners

Mastering Your Inner Potential

Creative Visualization

Manifesting With the Law of Attraction

Holistic Healing and Energy

Healing Animals with Reiki

Crystal Healing

Communicating with Your Spirit Guides

Empathic Understanding and Enlightenment

Being an Empath Today

Life on Fire

Healing Your Inner Child

Change Your Life

Raising Your Vibe

The Indie Author's Guides

The Indie Author's Guide to Fast Drafting Your Novel

Get a Handle on Life

Get a Handle on Stress

Time Bound

Get a Handle on Anxiety

Get a Handle on Depression

Get a Handle on Procrastination

The Holistic Yoga and Wellness Series

Yoga for Beginners

Yoga for Stress

Yoga for Back Pain

Yoga for Weight Loss

Yoga for Flexibility

Yoga for Advanced Beginners

Yoga for Fitness

Yoga for Runners

Yoga for Energy

Yoga for Your Sex Life

Yoga to Beat Depression and Anxiety

Yoga for Menstruation

Yoga to Detox Your Body

Yoga to Tone Your Body

The DIY Body Care Series

Creating Your Own Body Butter

Creating Your Own Body Scrub

Creating Your Own Body Spray

free

EMBRACING BALANCE
The Power of Gray Magic

MONIQUE JOINER SIEDLAK

WHEN YOU SUBSCRIBE

MOJOSIEDLAK.COM/MOONLIGHT-MUSINGS

SUPPORT ME BY LEAVING A REVIEW!

goodreads

amazon

BookBub

www.ingramcontent.com/pod-product-compliance
Lightning Source LLC
Chambersburg PA
CBHW060848050426
42453CB00008B/897